Summary of

Capitalist Technology fo

PHILIP VANDER

1. In a fully socialised economic system, the absence of market price signals prevents the central planners from discovering the relative scarcities of resources and the relative costs of their alternative uses.

2. A centrally-planned, collectivised economy cannot achieve an efficient allocation of *capital* because of its abolition of the risk-taking function of entrepreneurship.

3. The record of Soviet planning provides an instructive case study of the problems of socialist calculation and collectivist organisation, and confirms the early theoretical objections of market economists.

4. Just as black markets help to lubricate production and distribution and prevent the Soviet economy from seizing up completely, so world prices come to the rescue of Soviet planners by providing them with a rough benchmark by which to fix their prices.

5. Because of the absence of market incentives, the Soviet economy suffers from an inherent inability to generate significant domestic innovation.

6. The absence of property rights and general lack of financial autonomy for individuals and enterprises discourage risk-taking and inhibit experimentation.

7. The fundamental backwardness of the Soviet economy is reflected in low living standards, lack of choice, and widespread shortages of consumer goods.

8. Imported Western technology has compensated the Soviet system for some of its built-in defects, especially its inability to generate significant native innovation.

9. Western *civilian* technology has played an important rôle in promoting Soviet *military* programmes, releasing domestic Soviet resources for military uses, and facilitating internal repression.

10. Imported Western technology helps perpetuate Soviet totalitarianism by resolving its inner contradiction: how to obtain technical innovation without setting in motion a politically dangerous liberalisation of the Soviet economy.

Research Monograph 35 published (price £1.50) by

 THE INSTITUTE OF ECONOMIC AFFAIRS
2 Lord North Street, Westminster
London SW1P 3LB   Telephone: 01-799 3745

IEA PUBLICATIONS

Subscription Service

An annual subscription is the most convenient way to obtain our publications. Every title we produce in all our regular series will be sent to you immediately on publication and without further charge, representing a substantial saving.

*Subscription rates**

Britain: £15·00 p.a. including postage.

£14·00 p.a. if paid by Banker's Order.

£10·00 p.a. teachers and students who pay *personally*.

Europe and South America: £20 or equivalent.

Other countries: Rates on application. In most countries subscriptions are handled by local agents.

*These rates are *not* available to companies or to institutions.

To: The Treasurer, Institute of Economic Affairs,
2 Lord North Street,
Westminster, London SW1P 3LB.

I should like to subscribe beginning....................................
I enclose a cheque/postal order for:

☐ £15·00

☐ Please send me a Banker's Order form

☐ Please send me an Invoice

☐ £10·00 [I am a teacher/student at.............................]

Name...

Address..

....

Signed...................................... Date.................

RM/35

Capitalist Technology for Soviet Survival

PHILIP VANDER ELST

Published by
THE INSTITUTE OF ECONOMIC AFFAIRS
1981

First published March 1981

© THE INSTITUTE OF ECONOMIC AFFAIRS 1981

ISSN 0073-9103
ISBN 0-255 36140-8

Printed in Great Britain by
Goron Pro-Print Ltd., Churchill Industrial Estate, Lancing, Sussex
Set in Univers 9 on 11pt Series 689

Contents

4

Preface

IEA *Research Monographs* accommodate texts in which the main emphasis is normally on the research content, with implications and conclusions drawn from it.

Research Monograph 35 consists primarily of the evidence on the support given to the Russian economic system of centralised socialist or communist planning by technology bought or otherwise derived from Western capitalist countries. Mr Philip Vander Elst opens his review of the evidence with a discussion of the endemic defect of a centralised system in failing to generate its own technological innovation and dispose of it in the most efficient manner to the diverse uses to which it could be put. The evidence he assembles is derived from varied researches in Britain, the USA and elsewhere, though not from Russia itself, since secretiveness is a characteristic of a planned society, again endemic rather than accidental. The main impression left by this evidence, which Mr Vander Elst justifiably emphasises, is that whatever low rate of progress in economic development the Russian system can claim is due in no small measure to capitalist technology: without it, Russian production, income per head and living standards would be still lower, and the contrast with the output, income per head and living standards of capitalist countries even more compelling.

The assembly of evidence provokes the central issue raised by the *Monograph*: the policy of the capitalist West on socialist Russia. Mr Vander Elst rightly points to the essential dilemma of the centrally planned state: it must maintain control over economic activity if the political power of the central planners is to survive; but it must allow the people to use the information about local supply and demand that only they possess in conducting local private buying and selling in markets if living standards are not to sag and debilitated productive effort further weaken the political system.

Here Mr Vander Elst discusses the essence of his conclusion: he maintains that imported Western technology saves the Soviet leadership from the dilemma by raising living standards without allowing more than the minimal, politically-controlled, market activity. The Soviet leaders would then import capitalist technological expertise but continue their efforts to suppress knowledge of capitalist living standards, which may be more general than they would like but less than it would be with a free press and unrestricted international contacts. Mr Vander Elst believes that imported Western technology will enable the Soviet system to preserve its power for perhaps a further 60 years. The intriguing question is whether the importation of Western technology may merely postpone the day of reckoning and delay the withering away of Soviet socialism for only a decade or two to the end of the century.

So Mr Vander Elst's argument remains in principle: capitalist technology is prolonging Russian socialism. And he argues in support that trade between the West and Russia does not yield the classical advantage of liberal international exchange long refined by economists. He therefore calls upon statesmen as well as capitalists in the West to reconsider their thinking.

In his *Research Monograph* the author thus points to a dilemma for the West. Will the inevitable demise of socialism in Russia (and Poland and elsewhere in Eastern Europe) be unintentionally hastened by international exchange, as Britain now contemplates, despite the invasion of Afghanistan, by spreading knowledge of the West and inducing liberalising reforms of the socialist state? Or will the demise be better hastened by denying technology that for a period could prolong the socialist system?

The Institute has to thank two economists, with diverse approaches, Professor Alec Nove and Dr Ljubo Sirc, both of the University of Glasgow, for criticisms and suggestions that the author has borne in mind in his final revisions. The constitution of the Institute requires it to dissociate its Trustees, Directors and Advisers from the analyses of its authors, but it offers Mr Vander Elst's clearly argued *Research Monograph* as a timely discussion of a stubborn issue in East/West relations that requires more thought than it has been given.

January 1981   ARTHUR SELDON

The Author

PHILIP VANDER ELST was born in 1951 and educated at Bryanston School and the University of Oxford, where he read Politics, Philosophy and Economics. He has worked as a freelance journalist and on the staff of the Centre for Policy Studies, and is currently working as a researcher and writer for the IEA.

He has completed three lecture tours of the United States at the invitation of the US Industrial Council Education Foundation, and is a member of its advisory board. He is the author of a number of pamphlets published by USIC and the American Conservative Union, and has contributed articles to *Human Events* and the *American Spectator.*

Mr Vander Elst has also written and broadcasted religious programmes for BBC radio.

ONE

Introduction

This *Monograph* sets out to examine the basic organisational weaknesses of the Soviet economic system and the way they are counterbalanced by imported Western technology. The political dimension within which the Soviet economy operates is also briefly analysed because the central policy dilemmas facing the the Soviet leaders cannot otherwise be understood. The significance of Western technology to the USSR cannot be divorced from this political context. Totalitarian societies, by their very nature, cannot be studied intelligibly without consideration of political factors.

The *Monograph* begins with an analysis of the difficulties of socialist calculation and monopoly in the Soviet system, and discusses the failure of the Soviet authorities to resolve them satisfactorily. It emphasises the lack of economic progress in the USSR over the last half-century, despite the beneficial rôle of black markets in lubricating the Soviet economy and loosening the rigidities of Soviet central planning. Particular attention is drawn to the inherent inability of the Soviet economy to generate significant domestic innovation.

The question is then asked: How does the inefficient and poverty-stricken Soviet economy manage both to sustain itself in the first place, *and* support a vast and technologically sophisticated military sector? What explains the co-existence of chronic grain shortages and an ambitious Space programme?

An attempt is made to answer this question in terms of the rôle played by Western technological transfers in Soviet economic development since the 1920s. There is then a discussion of the pros and cons of East-West trade which is followed, in conclusion, by an attempt to derive some general but definite recommendations for Western policy.

TWO

The Dilemma of Socialist Calculation

The dilemma of socialist calculation was first raised in a major way by Professor Ludwig von Mises, in 1920. In his famous article,[1] Mises demonstrated that in an economy based on collective ownership and central planning—in which markets had been abolished—rational economic calculation of costs was impracticable.

Normally, in a free market economy based on private ownership, an entrepreneur must be aware of the precise possibilities for profit available to him if he employs his capital in a variety of ways. Consequently, if resources are to be allocated to their most efficient uses, relative prices must register the relative costs of employing the same quantity of scarce resources in different directions and combinations. Throughout the economy prices must therefore reflect 'opportunity costs', i.e. the cost of alternative uses foregone. But under a fully socialist system, i.e. one in which the private ownership of the means of production, distribution and exchange has been abolished, the absence of market price signals prevents the central planners from discovering the relative scarcities of resources and the relative costs of their alternative uses. Hence the organisation of production and distribution is bound to be irrational in a 'command economy'.

Inadequacy of socialist reply to Mises

It is widely held that Mises was successfully 'refuted' and the possibility of socialist calculation finally established by theorists like Oskar Lange[2] and Abba Lerner.[3] The latter, it is suggested, demonstrated the possibility of finding a practical solution to the problem of socialist calculation by the concept of 'market socialism'. Thus Lerner and Lange argued in favour of a system in which

---

[1] 'Economic Calculation in the Socialist Commonwealth', in F. A. Hayek (ed.), *Collectivist Economic Planning*, Routledge & Kegan Paul, London, 1935.

[2] Oskar Lange (with Fred M. Taylor), *On the Economic Theory of Socialism*, McGraw-Hill, New York, 1938.

[3] A. P. Lerner, 'Economic Theory and Socialist Economy', *Review of Economic Studies*, Vol. II, October 1934.

the central planning board would arrive at market clearing prices by trial and error. Unfortunately this reply has derived its apparent effectiveness from its very concession to Mises's essential theoretical criticism. The American economist, Paul Craig Roberts, has put it:

> 'Lange refutes Mises by utilising the market mechanism and the value criteria it generates—precisely the mechanism and values that were to be replaced under socialism by a planning mechanism—the impossibility of which was the contention of Mises.'[1]

Furthermore, a centrally planned collectivist economy cannot achieve an efficient allocation of *capital* because of its abolition of the function of entrepreneurship.

No substitute for the entrepreneur

It is perhaps theoretically conceivable that in an imaginary world in which all economic change had ceased, a group of central planners (armed with the necessary computers) would be able to organise a rational structure for *existing* production.[2] But how would this be possible in the real world of incessant economic change? How can the planners know which are the most fruitful outlets for capital investment in the absence of profit and loss signals? How can these profit and loss signals exist in an economy without investors and entrepreneurs, able and willing to risk their resources in new ventures or on untried ideas? These objections were raised by Mises, in his book, *Human Action*:

> 'In a free market economy the entrepreneurs and capitalists establish corporations and other firms, enlarge or reduce their size, dissolve them or merge them with other enterprises; they grant, withdraw, and recover credits; in short they perform all those acts the totality of which is called the capital and money market. It is these financial transactions of promoters and speculators that direct production into those channels in which it satisfies the most urgent wants of the consumers in the best possible way. . . .

---

[1] 'The Polycentric Soviet Economy', *Journal of Law and Economics*, Vol. XII, April 1969.

[2] 'A rational structure of production' means, in this context, not only that it embodies *technical* efficiency, i.e. the cost-effective management of particular units of labour, capital and raw materials to produce particular goods whose output has been predetermined. It also embodies the notion of *economic* efficiency, resulting from the allocation of resources to satisfy demand. Economic efficiency thus entails the harmonious co-ordination of supply and demand among millions of interacting decisions in supply and demand. It describes an economic system whose internal organisation is adapted to the myriad preferences of consumers, freely expressed through market-clearing prices.

Nobody has ever suggested that the socialist commonwealth could invite the promoters and speculators to continue their speculations and then deliver their profits to the common chest. . . . One cannot *play* speculation and investment. The speculators and investors expose their own wealth, their own destiny. This fact makes them responsible to the consumers . . . If one relieves them of this responsibility, one deprives them of their very character.'[1]

Lionel Robbins has argued that Mises, by asserting the *impossibility* of socialist calculation, overstated his case since collectivist systems have produced 'vast quantities of stuff which, whether or not it corresponded to the von Mises ideal of rationality, had *some* use for *some* purposes'.[2] But Lord Robbins implicitly rebuts his own objection by acknowledging the possible confict between Mises's 'ideal of rationality' and the pattern of production prevailing in collectivist states. Mises argued that a collectivist system could not establish a production structure that was 'rational' in the sense of satisfying ordinary *consumer* preferences—as opposed to the restricted objectives of an all-powerful political oligarchy. This judgement has been amply confirmed by experience.

The liquidation of the entrepreneur, as a result of collectivisation, represents an insuperable element in the dilemma of socialist calculation, but it is not the only one. An allied flaw is that a centrally controlled system suffers from inherent organisational inefficiency because of the absence of the commercial pressures arising out of competition.

The disadvantages of socialist monopoly

The existence of an archipelago of state monopolies within a collectivist economy not only imposes the obvious costs flowing from a lack of accountability to consumers; it also creates two other major difficulties. The first concerns the relationship between the central planning authorities and the individual state enterprises that are supposed to implement the plans handed down from above. The second is the marriage between economic and political power.

(i) *Conflicting objectives*

The absence of a genuine market mechanism of competitive pricing deprives the various state enterprises of the necessary criteria for autonomous action. Moreover, the inability of an over-

---

[1] Henry Regnery, Chicago, 1966, pp. 707-709.

[2] *Political Economy Past and Present,* Macmillan, 1976, p. 144.

burdened central planning board to absorb and utilise the mass of information necessary for the central co-ordination of millions of costs, prices, and production plans requires essential decision-making to be delegated to other planning bodies. The result is a chaos of conflicting requests and instructions instead of a clear, coherent, and internally consistent set of guidelines to which state enterprises can adapt their activity. The more complex and numerous the interactions within a developing industrialised economy, the worse this dilemma of central planning becomes. There is also the additional difficulty that it is in the interests of individual Soviet enterprises to provide the authorities with inexact information (pp. 17-19).

The Hungarian economist, Professor Tibor Liska, has commented succinctly on the difficulties facing the managers of state enterprises:

> 'The intricacy of economic life follows . . . from the fact that hosts of contrary tendencies must be brought into harmony with optimum efficiency. The stricter and more rigid the regulations proscribing the enforcement of such contrary tendencies, the more contradictory the directives must become. One receiving the directives has but a single choice: *not to observe all the directives.*'[1]

(ii) *Dominance of politics over economics*

The second difficulty created by collectivisation results from the consequent marriage between economic and political power. It produces a system in which economic rationality plays a subordinate rôle to the political goal of power maximisation in the motivation of the central planners. Nepotism, political loyalty and the imperatives of propaganda characteristically override considerations of equity and efficiency. This has been the experience of numerous communist economies, especially that of the Soviet Union. In 1969, for instance, in the Soviet republic of Azerbaidjan, a comprehensive range of state and party offices could be bought by those with the appropriate party connections.[2] In addition, the American economist, Dr Gary North, has written:

> 'Politics, rather than economics, has dominated Soviet production plans for decades. Naum Jasny has argued that the very planning units—the Five Year Plans—were originally propaganda devices, and that the

---

[1] Quoted in P. C. Roberts's 'The Polycentric Soviet Economy', *op. cit.*

[2] The 'going rates' were as follows: First Secretary of a party district committee: 200,000 roubles; Second Secretary: 100,000 roubles; chairman of a collective farm: 50,000 roubles; factory manager: 10-15,000 roubles; director of an institute: 40,000 roubles; director of a theatre or opera house: 10-30,000 roubles. (Professor Ilja Zemtsov, *La Corruption en Union Soviétique*, Hachette, Paris, 1976, p. 78.)

annual and quarterly plans were the real basis for planning; this, he says, prevailed until the advent of the Seven Year Plans, which came in the mid-1950s. . . . The goals of the 1930s were set so high that it would have been impossible for any régime to have reached them . . . Planning for long-term goals was a function not of economic realities but rather of oratory.'[1]

---

[1] Gary North, 'The Crisis in Soviet Economic Planning', *Modern Age*, Vol. 14, No. 1, Winter 1969-70, p. 51. Also Dr Naum Jasny, *Soviet Industrialisation 1928-52*, University of Chicago Press, 1961, pp. 25-27.

THREE

The Failure of Soviet Planning

The record of Soviet economic planning provides an instructive case study of the problems of socialist calculation and collectivist organisation. There now exists a mass of evidence from Soviet and other sources which illustrates in practice the theoretical difficulties analysed by the economists.

Impossibility of central control

The statistical impossibility of detailed control of the economy from the centre was implied in the warnings about the future of the Soviet system uttered in 1964 by Victor M. Glushkov, then head of the Soviet Union's research programme in cybernetics. He estimated that the planning bureaucracy of the Soviet Union would have to grow *36-fold by 1980* if Soviet planning methods were not radically reformed. He further estimated that, even if high-speed computers were used, performing 30,000 operations per second, it would require a million computers working without interruption for several years to plan the entire economy. Nor is this a surprising calculation given that, according to Professor G. Warren Nutter, the total number of economic relationships within the Soviet Union approach several quintillion.[1] Furthermore, since the economy is forever changing, the data fed into the computers would require continual revision, with the result that the planners could never catch up with events. Consequently, even Glushkov's alarming calculation underestimates the magnitude of the task facing the Soviet planners.

Centralised *versus* decentralised planning: the problem of balance

Given the obvious truth that the Soviet central planners are not omniscient, periodic attempts have been made in the USSR to decentralise the planning process in order to achieve the desired integration, into the central plan, of the on-the-spot knowledge

---

[1] Reported by Leon Smolinski, 'What Next in Soviet Planning?', *Foreign Affairs*, Vol. XLII, 1964.

of local managers.[1] In 1963, Gosplan, the Soviet central planning agency, directly controlled about 18,000 products, most of which were aggregations of hundreds or even thousands of sub-products.[2] Responsibility for directing the activities of the Soviet economy was shared between hundreds of state and party agencies. Today, Gosplan controls the allocation of about 2,000 inputs, while other bodies allocate another 38,000. Although there has been a constant shift in the locus of Soviet planning, the continuing tension between centralised ministerial planning and localised decision-making has inevitable remained. Thus Professor Alec Nove has written:

> 'the authorities that hand down plans are often unaware of the tasks already given that enterprise by other authorities.'[3]

This comment is supported by a statement by Mr. I. Borovitsky, a disgruntled enterprise manager, which appeared in *Pravda* on 5 October 1962:

> 'The department of Gosplan which drafts the production programme for *Sovnarkhozy* regional economic councils and enterprises is totally uninterested in costs or profits. Ask the senior official in the production programme department in what factory it is cheaper to produce this or that commodity? He has no idea, and never even puts the question to himself. He is responsible only for the distribution of production tasks.
> Another department, not really concerned with costs of production, decides on the plan for gross output.
> A third department or sub-department, proceeding from the principle that costs must also decline and labour productivity increase, plans costs, wages fund and labour on the basis of past performance. Material allocations and components are planned by numerous other departments. Not a single department of Gosplan is responsible for the consistency of these plans.'

Black markets to the rescue

The 'planned chaos' of the Soviet system (to use a phrase coined by Mises) has been partially mitigated by widespread illegal trading between Soviet enterprises, a phenomenon known as 'blat'.[4] Because supply channels are plagued by delays and

---

[1] These attempts, and the pressures behind them, were described by Dr Margaret Miller in *The Rise of the Russian Consumer*, IEA, 1965.

[2] Peter Wiles and Leon Smolinski, 'The Soviet Planning Pendulum', *Problems of Communism*, Vol. XII, (USIA), November-December, 1963, p. 21.

[3] *The Soviet Economy: An Introduction*, Praeger, New York, 1966, p. 207.

[4] Described by Joseph S. Berliner in *Factory and Manager in the USSR*, Harvard University Press, Cambridge, Mass., 1957, Chapters 11 and 12. Also Margaret Miller, *op. cit.*, especially Chapter 3.

frequently deliver the wrong or inferior goods, managers have been compelled to seek alternative sources of materials in order to meet production quotas. Failure to fulfil the requirements imposed by the planning authorities not only puts their bonuses and promotions at risk, but may even threaten their livelihood and their liberty. Hence the energetic participation in black market activities throughout the Soviet economy.

There is, however, another important motive behind black market activity in the Soviet Union: the desire of most Soviet citizens to supplement their extremely low official incomes and living standards (pp. 22 and 25-27) through illegal speculation. Particular emphasis is laid on this factor by unofficial Soviet sources, which insist on the universality of popular involvement in black market transactions.[1]

How does the black market operate? A plant may have a surplus of its product in any given year because the manager overstated his supply needs or understated the productive capacity of his plant in the previous year, when the central plans were drawn up. As a result, the manager may trade his surplus goods to another firm (or factory) in exchange for some future service or present luxury. Such black market operations may help smaller enterprises on a lower priority list for supplies as well as the high priority industries during crises. The organisation of black market transactions is carried out by 'middlemen' (called *tolkatchi*) with informal connections, employed under bogus administrative titles. These *tolkatchi* co-ordinate the underground facilities of supply and demand and thrive in what Berliner calls 'an economic soil watered by shortages and fertilised by unrealistic targets'.[2]

World prices to the (planners') rescue

Just as black markets help to lubricate production and distribution and so prevent the Soviet economy from seizing up completely, so world prices come to the rescue of Soviet planners by providing

---

[1] Vladimir Bukovsky, in his autobiography, *To Build A Castle* (André Deutsch, London, 1978), writes: 'Wages are beggarly and everyone steals as much as he can. Is it that the authorities don't know? Of course they know. And they even prefer it that way. A man who steals isn't in a position to make demands. And if he does become so bold, he can easily be put away for theft. Everyone is guilty.'

As if to confirm Bukovsky's comments, Moscow Radio (30 November 1977) quoted these words of a 'big-time thief' awaiting trial: 'Everyone steals, but not many get caught, so why should I be the one who gets into trouble?'

[2] Berliner, *op. cit.*

them with a rough benchmark by which to fix their prices. Thus the Soviet Union and other communist countries are not completely socialised since they continue to operate within a world market. This truth is generally acknowledged today and is amusingly illustrated by Professor Peter Wiles, describing an encounter with Polish communist planners:

> 'What actually happens is that "world prices", i.e. *capitalist world prices,* are used in all intra-block trade. They are translated into roubles . . . and entered in bilateral clearing accounts. To the question, "What would you do if there were no capitalist world?" came only the answer "We'll cross that bridge when we come to it".'[1]

---

[1] 'Changing Economic Thought in Poland', *Oxford Economic Papers,* Vol. 9, June 1957, pp. 202-3.

FOUR

The Soviet Economic Record

The paucity of Soviet innovation

World prices and black markets notwithstanding, the Soviet economy remains gravely defective in its performance. In addition to the flaws examined, the Soviet economy suffers from an inherent inability to generate significant domestic innovation. The reasons all relate to its system of collectivisation and central planning.

First, the heavily bureaucratised system frustrates, by its very nature, the rapid collection, digestion and dissemination of information relevant to the application of technical invention to industrial processes.

Secondly, the general lack of financial and ideological autonomy for individuals and enterprises, combined with the prevailing psychological pressure to conform and refrain from upsetting superiors, discourages risk-taking and inhibits experimentation. Furthermore, the absence of property rights deprives Soviet citizens of a personal stake in the economic fruits of innovation.

Thus, while there is nothing necessarily lacking in the quality of Soviet scientific research, there are no incentives, and therefore no market-type mechanism, by which the fruits of research can be systematically tested against competing alternatives and then incorporated into the economy. Weapons innovation, however, can more easily be achieved by a centralised bureaucracy since this type of innovation is predicated upon more easily defined objectives.

'Military planners, unlike economic planners, can estimate fairly accurately what the next technological stage will be for a given weapon and can define a technical objective for that weapon in clear terms. Work towards such a pre-ordained objective can proceed along well-established lines'.[1]

Western origins of Soviet technology

The paucity of Soviet innovation has been amply documented by an American economist, Dr Antony Sutton. In his exhaustive

---

[1] Antony Sutton, *Western Technology and Soviet Economic Development 1917-1965*, Vol. 3, 1973, p. 361.

study, *Western Technology and Soviet Economic Development 1917-1965*,[1] Dr Sutton reveals that indigenous Soviet innovation has been practically nil since 1917. Between 1917 and 1930 there were no successful advances in any industry. From 1930 to 1945 there were some advances in the development of machine guns, synthetic rubber, oil drilling techniques, and boilers, but they were temporary and later abandoned in favour of foreign designs and processes. Between 1945 and 1965 most of the progress of Soviet innovation depended on the 'scaling up' of existing plants and technologies imported and copied from the West. ('Scaling up' means adaptive innovation. Thus the Soviets take a classic Western process and proceed by dint of investment, research and development to increase the size or capacity of the productive unit.) This was particularly so in iron and steel making, electricity generation and rocket technology.

Dr Sutton has examined 75 major technological processes in such crucial and diverse sectors as mining, oil, chemicals, machine building, aircraft, communications, agricultural equipment, etc., and estimated the percentage that originated in Russia. The startling results: between 1917 and 1930, 0 per cent; between 1930 and 1945, 10 per cent; between 1945 and 1965, 11 per cent (Tables 1-3).

Table 1 identifies the technological origins of industrial processes in 15 major Soviet industrial sectors between 1917 and 1965. Where Soviet innovation is the main process in use, it is noted in capitalised italics.

Low living standards

The fundamental weaknesses of the Soviet economic system coupled with the relative helplessness of the Soviet consumer in the face of the concentrated power of the party and state organs have reflected themselves in low living standards, lack of choice, and multitudinous shortages of consumer goods for ordinary Soviet citizens. Vladimir Bukovsky has said, 'wages are beggarly';[2] authorities like Professor Sergei Prokopovich, Dr Naum Jasny, and Mrs Janet Chapman[3] have concluded that the real wages of Soviet industrial workers in 1970 were hardly higher than in 1913.

[*continued on page 25*]

---

[1] Hoover Institution, Stanford, Calif., Vol. 1: *1917-1930*, 1968; Vol. 2: *1930-1945*, 1971; Vol. 3: *1945-1965*, 1973.

[2] *Op. cit.* (p. 19, footnote 1).

[3] *Real Wages in Soviet Russia since 1928*, Harvard University Press, 1963.

CHEMICAL INDUSTRIES

No.	Industrial Process	1917-1930	1930-1945	1945-1965
20	Basic acids	US/German/ Italian	US/German	UK
21	Basic alkalis	Tsarist/US	US/German/ UK/Tsarist/ Swedish	US/German
22	Fertilizers	Swedish/US/ German	Swedish	US/Belgian/ Dutch/Italian/ UK/Japanese
23	Synthetic fibre intermediates	French	French/ German	UK/German/ US
24	Agricultural pesticides	—	—	UK
25	Synthetic rubber	Tsarist	*SOVIET*	German/US/ UK
26	Rubber tyres	US/German	US/UK	US/UK/ Italian
27	Glass	US/German	Belgian/US	UK
28	Cement mills	Danish/ German	Danish/ German	Danish/French/ German
29	Coke by-products	Tsarist	US/German	Scaling-up
30	Pharmaceuticals	German	German/US	US/Austrian

MACHINE BUILDING

No.	Industrial Process	1917-1930	1930-1945	1945-1965
31	General technical assistance	German/UK	US/German	(None)
32	Machine tools	German/US	US/German/ UK	US/German
33	Ball bearings	Swedish/ Italian/ German	Italian/US	US/Italian
34	Instrumentation	US/German	US/German	US/German

ELECTRICAL EQUIPMENT

No.	Industrial Process	1917-1930	1930-1945	1945-1965
35	General technical assistance	US/German/ UK/German	US/UK	(None)
36	Heavy electrical equipment	US/UK/ German	US/UK	US/Scaling-up
37	Low tension equipment	US/Swedish/ French	US/German	German
38	Instruments	German/US	US/German	US/German

Table 1:
Technological Origins of Main Soviet Industrial Processes, 1917 to 1965

No.	Industrial Process	1917-1930	1930-1945	1945-1965
	MINING			
1	Underground equipment	German	US/German	US/UK/ German
2	Excavation equipment	German US/UK	US	US/UK/ German
3	Crushers	US	US	US
4	Ore beneficiation	—	US/ Swedish	US/German/ French
5	Sintering	—	US	US
	OIL INDUSTRY			
6	Drilling	US	*SOVIET*	*SOVIET*
7	Pumping	US	US	US
8	Pipelines: pipe	US/German	US	German/ Japanese
9	Pipelines: compressors	US/UK	US	US/Swiss
10	Refining and cracking	US/ German/UK	US	US/French/ German/ Czechoslovak
	FERROUS METALLURGY			
11	Pig iron	Classic blast furnace	Scaling-up	*SOVIET*/US/ German
12	Steelmaking	Classic open hearth	Scaling-up	Austrian/ *SOVIET*
13	Steel rolling: blooming	US/German	US/German	US/German
14	Steel rolling: wide sheets	US	US	US
15	Steel rolling: tubes	US/German	US	US
16	Continuous casting	US/German	US/German	German/ *SOVIET*
	NON-FERROUS METALLURGY			
17	Nickel smelting and refining	—	Canadian	Canadian/ Norwegian
18	Aluminium smelting and refining	German/US	US/*SOVIET*	*SOVIET*/US/ Czechoslovak
19	Copper smelting and refining	US	US	US

No.	Industrial Process	1917-1930	1930-1945	1945-1965
	SHIPBUILDING			
57	Hull construction	German	75 per cent foreign-built	66 per cent foreign-built
	Engine design:			
58	diesel	German	German	Danish/German/ Swiss
59	steam turbine	UK/US	UK	Not known
60	gas turbine	—	—	French
61	Trawlers	—	UK/French/ German	UK/German
62	Oceanographic equipment	—	US/German	US/Japanese
	AIRCRAFT			
63	Aircraft	German	US/Italian	*SOVIET*(?)
	Aircraft engines:			
64	internal combustion	US/German	US/French	—
65	turboprop	—	—	
66	pure jet	—	—	UK/German
67	Helicopters	—	*SOVIET*/Italian	*SOVIET*(?)
68	Landing and communication equipment	Not investigated	US	UK/US
	MILITARY INDUSTRIES			
69	Explosives	German	US	
70	Poison gas	German	US	
71	Tanks	French/UK/ Italian	US/UK/ *SOVIET*	Data classified
72	Machine guns	Tsarist/UK	*SOVIET*/ Finnish	
73	Submarines	German	German/UK	
74	Destroyers	—	Italian/French	
	CONSUMER INDUSTRIES			
75	Clothing industries	Tsarist/US/ German	UK/German	UK/German/ US
76	Boots and shoes	Austrian/ Danish	Not known	UK

Sources: Column 1—Sutton 1: *Western Technology . . . 1917 to 1930;* Column 2—Sutton 2: *Western Technology . . . 1930 to 1945;* Column 3—Sutton 3: *Western Technology . . . 1945 to 1965.*

Notes: (1) Multi-country listings indicate several technical origins, listed in order of relative importance.
(2) In a few cases, as for example in the origin of steam locomotives in the 1930-65 period, there has been Soviet adaptation of basic foreign or Tsarist-era designs; these entries are noted *SOVIET* first and foreign sources second.

No.	Industrial Process	1917-1930	1930-1945	1945-1965
	COMMUNICATIONS			
39	Telephone	Swedish/ French/US	Not investigated	French
40	Telegraph	Danish/UK	Danish	Not investigated
41	Radio	US	US	Not investigated
42	Television	—	US (black and white)	French (colour)/ German
43	Computers	—	—	US/UK
	PRIME MOVERS			
44	Steam boilers	Latvian/ German	*SOVIET*/US	US/UK/ German
45	Internal combustion	US	US	US/German
46	Diesel engines	German	German/UK	German/Danish/ US/Swiss
47	Gas turbines	—	—	French
	AGRICULTURAL EQUIPMENT			
48	Tractors	US/German	US	US/UK/ German
49	Cotton pickers	—	US	US
50	Seeding equipment	Tsarist	US	US/German
	TRANSPORTATION INDUSTRIES			
51	Automobile and trucks	Tsarist/US/ Italian	US	US/German/ Italian/French
52	Railroad locomotives:			
53	steam	Tsarist/ German/UK	Tsarist/US/ UK	*SOVIET*/US/ German
54	diesel-electric	US/German	German	US
55	electric	German/US	US/German	French/US
56	hydraulic	—	—	Austrian/ German

Table 2:
Summary Statement of the Origins of Soviet Technology from 1917 to 1965

Number of Major Technologies examined: 75 (in three time-slots)

	1	2	3	4	5	6
Period	Determined as all Soviet origin	Percentage of total examined	Determined as of both Soviet and Western origins	Percentage of total examined	Total (column 1 and 3)	Percentage of total
1917 to 1930	0	0	0	0	0	0
1930 to 1945	2	3	5	7	7	10
1945 to 1965	3	4	5	7	8	11

Source: Table 1.

Table 3:
Indigenous Soviet Innovation, 1917 to 1965

1917-1930	1930-1945	1945-1965
Primitive tractors	Turbodrill	Electro-drill
	Alumina from nepheline	Aircraft
	Synthetic rubber; SK-B	Sputnik
	Once-through boiler	Medical sutures
	Machine guns	Electro-slag welding
		'Scaling up'

Source: Sutton, op. cit., Vol. 3, Tables 25-2 and 29-1.

The Swiss economist, Jovan Pavlevski,[1] calculated (in 1969) that the real wages of Soviet industrial workers attained the level of 1913 only in 1963. He also found that the real incomes of Soviet agricultural workers in 1969 were only 1·2 per cent higher than in 1913.

The constant shortage in the Soviet Union of basic necessaries like washing powder, razor blades, meat and vegetables, and many other items,[2] reinforces the impression that average living standards have shown little advance over 1913.

Poverty in the Soviet Union

This picture of generally low living standards is further strengthened by evidence of widespread poverty among old people and the inhabitants of some of the more backward Soviet republics. Thus according to one Soviet expert, Ilja Zemtsov, formerly professor of sociology at the Lenin Institute of Baku (Azerbaidjan), one in two retired persons in the USSR lives in poverty.[3] Furthermore, in the Soviet republic of Azerbaidjan, 75 per cent of the population lives 'below the poverty line' and there are more homes without water, electricity and w.c.s than in the whole of Western Europe.[4] Some authorities calculate that about half of all housing in the Soviet Union is without running water or sewerage. Living space per person, in the mid-1970s, was only 11 square metres (approximately 120 sq. ft.) throughout the USSR, about *half* that available in Western Europe.[5]

Comparative living standards

Comparative living standards between ordinary Soviet workers and their counterparts in North America and Western Europe are indicated in Table 4 which compares the approximate worktime required for an average manufacturing employee to buy commodities in retail stores in Washington DC, in London, and at official state prices in Moscow, during May 1976. Living standards

---

[1] His findings are in *Economies et Sociétés* (journal of the Institute of Applied Economic Sciences, Geneva), February 1969.

[2] Below, Table 4, note (b), p. 26, and footnote 2, pp. 55-56.

[3] *La Corruption en Union Sovietique, op. cit.,* p. 117. Professor Zemtsov emigrated to Israel in 1973.

[4] *Ibid.,* pp. 47 and 93.

[5] Svetozar Pejovich, *Life in the Soviet Union: A Report Card On Socialism*, the Fisher Institute, Dallas, Texas, 1979, p. 55; W. S. Smith, 'Housing in the Soviet Union', in *Soviet Economic Prospects for the Seventies*, Joint Economic Committee, US Congress, Washington DC, 1973, p. 405.

Table 4:
Comparative Standards of Living Expressed in Worktime:[a] Washington DC, London and Moscow, May 1976

(Worktime is in minutes, unless otherwise stated)

Commodity	Washington DC	London	Moscow
Milk (1 litre)	7	11	21
Hamburger meat, beef (1 Kg.)	34	76	3·5 hours
Sausages, pork (1 Kg.)	71	60	2·6 hours
Potatoes (1 Kg.)	8	23	(7)[b]
Apples, eating (1 Kg.)	16	24	5·4 hours
Sugar (1 Kg.)	9	15	65
White bread (1 Kg.)	21	10	20
Eggs (10)	10	13	97
Vodka (0·7 litres)	67	3·4 hours	9·8 hours
Cigarettes (20)	10	27	23
Weekly food basket for four people	17·2 hours	28·2 hours	64·6 hours
Soap, toilet (150 gram.)	5	10	72
Lipstick	31	54	7·8 hours
Panty hose	17	15	9 hours
Men's shoes (black leather)	6·7 hours	7·7 hours	36 hours
Man's business suit	25 hours	40 hours	106 hours
Refrigerator, small (150 litres)	47 hours	50 hours	168 hours
Colour TV set, large (59cm screen)	3·9 weeks	5·5 weeks	19·5 weeks
Small car (Fiat or Zhiguli)	6·9 months	11·1 months	3·1 years

Source: Radio Liberty Research Supplement, 16 June 1976.

a Worktime is based on *average take-home pay* of male and female manufacturing workers. Income taxes, social security taxes (US and UK), and health insurance premiums (US only) have been deducted from wages; family allowances (UK and USSR) have been added. A worker is assumed to have three dependants. In dollars, hourly take-home pay in January 1976 was $3·83 for American workers, $1·83 for British workers, and $1·10 for Russian workers.

b Many commodities are subject to periodic shortages in the Soviet Union; an example was the previous year's crop of potatoes in Moscow in May 1976. Expressed in worktime, the regular price for a kilo (about 2·2 pounds) of old potatoes would have been seven minutes—if any had been available. New potatoes also were not available in the state-run stores but could be bought for 72-minutes' worth of worktime in *kolkhoz* markets (where collective farmers are allowed to sell produce from their small gardens). Apples likewise were unavailable in state stores, but a kilo could be bought in kolkhoz markets for the money earned from about 5½ hours' work.

in Moscow, low as they are, have been artificially boosted above the national level since the early 1930s for largely propagandist purposes. According to Alexander Solzhenitsyn (who spent 55 years in the remoter areas of the USSR before he was exiled in 1974), Moscow, in material comfort,

'is almost as superior to the rest of the Soviet Union as the West is superior to Moscow. . . . Authentic Soviet life is to be seen only in provincial towns, in rural areas, in the labour camps and in the harsh conditions of the peacetime army'.[1]

Some Russian provincial towns 'have not seen meat, butter or eggs for decades'.[2]

The Tsarist legacy

The question often arises whether the low living standards of the average Soviet citizen are not largely due to an inherited legacy of economic backwardness. Did not Soviet industrialisation have to start from scratch?

Whilst pre-revolutionary Russia was backward compared to Britain, Germany, or the United States, she left behind an already advanced industrial base for the Soviets to build upon. Dr Sutton states:

'There is evidence that by 1916 Tsarist Russia had industrial units on a scale and utilising a technology equal to that anywhere in the world. . . . pre-revolutionary indigenous Russian innovation was apparent in the beet sugar industry, in aluminium smelting (Bayer), in synthetic rubber (Ostrimilensky), and in automobiles and aircraft (Sikorsky).'[3]

During 18 of the last 25 pre-1914 years, Russia enjoyed the highest rate of industrial growth in the world. By 1913 she was overtaking France as the world's fourth industrial power; in the 1890s her industrial production had been only one-third that of France. Between 1893 and 1913 her coal production increased five-fold and her iron-ore and cast-iron production four-fold. Oil production, railway mileage and grain production doubled.[4] By 1913, Tsarist Russia held second place in the world in oil production and third place in railway construction and the manufacture

---

[1] 'Misconceptions About Russia Are A Threat To America', *Foreign Affairs* (ed. William P. Bundy), Spring 1980, New York, pp. 811-812.

[2] *Ibid.,* p. 813.

[3] Sutton, Vol. 3, p. 409; also Vol. 1, pp. 183-4.

[4] At the turn of the century, grain was the major export of Tsarist Russia. About a quarter of the total crop was exported in a normal year. This contrasts with the poor contemporary performance of collectivised Soviet agriculture (p. 28) and the continual dependence on imported grain.

of cotton. The growth in industrial production over the last 40-odd years of the Tsarist period was more than during most of the post-revolutionary period. Thus the growth of industrial production averaged 5·3 per cent per annum from 1870 to 1913, and 4·4 per cent per annum between 1913 and 1955.[1]

Despite these foundations, established before the revolution, an official American estimate suggested that as late as 1970 the USSR ranked only 20th in the world in output per head.[2] The legacy of the past is obviously not a convincing explanation of the Soviet Union's poor economic performance since 1917.

The costs of Soviet collectivism

The analysis so far indicates, on the contrary, that the true explanation of Soviet backwardness lies in her distinctive system of social and economic organisation. The dilemma of socialist calculation, the liquidation of the entrepreneur, the lack of normal commercial pressures and incentives, and so on, are the consequences of the twin policies of central planning and collectivisation. These, in turn, result from the attempt to realise Marxist ideology in Russian conditions. This conclusion receives striking support from the now legendary failure of collectivised agriculture in the Soviet Union.

One-third of the country's total agricultural output is provided by the tiny *private* holdings cultivated by Soviet collective farmers in their spare time. Over one-half of this output consists of livestock products, but since the livestock is neither fed nor pastured on these private holdings, it is arguably possible to overstate the superiority of the private sector by neglecting this qualification. On the other hand, the right of Soviet farmers to *own* one cow, two pigs, and as many chickens as they want (per household), and the personal incentive this provides for their own economic activity, are the key elements in explaining the disproportionate productiveness of the private sector and its superiority over collectivised agriculture. These private holdings, moreover, account for only about 3 per cent of the total agricultural area of the Soviet Union. On average, private holdings supply about 44 per cent of the total income of collective farmers—in cash and kind.[3]

---

[1] Professor G. Warren Nutter, *The Growth of Industrial Production in the Soviet Union*, Princeton University Press, Princeton, N.J., for the National Bureau of Economic Research, 1962, pp. 164-5 and p. 285.

[2] *Hearings before the Subcommittee on Strategic Arms Limitation Talks*, US Senate, Washington DC, 1970.

[3] Svetozar Pejovich, *op. cit.*, p. 94.

It is arguable that the economic costs of Soviet collectivism cannot be limited to poor living standards and inefficient agriculture. What about the economic impact of numerous purges and political struggles, such as the war against the 'kulaks'[1] in the 1930s? What have been the broad economic consequences of the bloodletting brought about by the Soviet leadership's abuse of its monopoly power?

Scholars have produced estimates which suggest that anything between 20 and 66 million Russians have died in *internal repression* since 1917.[2] If these estimates are even remotely accurate, they must be regarded as having had a significant bearing on the performance of the Soviet economy over half a century. At the very least, allowance must be made for the adverse consequences over the years of the large-scale destruction of the labour force —especially the liquidation of skilled scientific, technical and managerial personnel. The 'opportunity costs' of this human tragedy are incalculable.

What is the answer to the Soviet riddle?

We now face the billion rouble question: How can all the analysis (and evidence) of Soviet poverty, backwardness, and inefficiency be reconciled with the apparent evidence of the USSR's military super-power status? How can semi-Asiatic stagnation co-exist with the latest military and rocket technology?

The Soviet riddle is partly explained by the obvious truth that any large centrally-controlled state is capable (at an immense price and to the neglect of everything else) of concentrating all its resources on a few selected strategic sectors. But the most

---

[1] The wealthier peasants. The Soviet régime was undiscriminating in its campaigns against the peasantry and was consequently resisted by the poorer peasants as much as by the kulaks.

[2] The late Professor Tibor Szamuely: 'The cost purely in terms of human lives sacrificed on the altar of "Socialism", *excluding* losses in the Civil War of 1918-21 and the Second World War, or the consequent decline in the birth rate, is no less than twenty million souls.' (Postscript to Tufton Beamish, *Half-Marx*, Tom Stacey, 1970.) Robert Conquest, in *The Great Terror*, calculates that 20 million Russians died in Stalin's purges *alone*. In his later study, *The Human Cost of Soviet Communism*, commissioned by the US Senate in 1971, Mr Conquest estimated that a minimum of 35 million people had died since 1917 as a result of Communist oppression. The figure of 66 million dead was established by the Russian statistician, Professor Kurganov, in a study published in *Novie Rousskoie Slova*, Paris, 14 April 1964. Kurganov's calculation was based on official Soviet demographic statistics. His figure is quoted by Solzhenitsyn in *The Gulag Archipelago*, Vol. 2, Fontana-Collins, 1976, p. 10.

important part of the explanation lies in an altogether different direction: in the massive transfer to the USSR of technology from the market-oriented economies of the United States and Western Europe. This assertion is justified on two grounds:

(i) the progress that can be achieved by concentrating resources in a few key sectors remains limited, given the inherent obstacles to innovation resulting from the absence of property rights, autonomy and incentives;

(ii) much innovation of military use originates in the civilian sector, from commercial developments designed to satisfy consumers (below, pp. 46-47).

But the concentration of resources on the military sector starves the civilian sector and reinforces the inbuilt deterrents to civilian innovation that already exist. As a result, the military benefits achieved by this process are partly counterbalanced by the consequent loss of civilian technology with a military potential.

The rest of this *Monograph* attempts to describe the Soviet importation of Western technology and to analyse its rôle in compensating the Soviet system for its built-in organisational defects, especially its inability to generate significant native innovation. (pp. 21-22 and Tables 1-3, pp. 23-24).

Soviet support for technological transfer hypothesis

Although the record of Soviet technological dependence on foreign sources is largely expunged from official Soviet writing, isolated statements let the cat out of the bag. Thus the Soviet journal, *Foreign Trade*, in 1977 said the USSR

'efficiently uses the benefits of the international division of labour and constantly imports technically advanced plant and the latest licences and know-how'.

Similarly, at the Twenty-third Congress of the Communist Party of the Soviet Union (CPSU) in 1966, the report on the directives delivered by Kosygin stated:

'The Soviet Union is going to buy . . . over a thousand sets of equipment for enterprises and shops in the chemical, light, food and other industries. Deliveries from the fraternal countries [i.e. Eastern Europe] will cover 48% of our needs in sea-going freighters, 40% . . . in main line and industrial electric locomotives, about 36% . . . in railway cars.'

Since the Soviet definition of 'sets of equipment' means complete plant installations, and the period covered was five years, the magnitude of the planned assistance may be readily seen. Moreover, as Eastern Europe has been communist only since the late

1940s, it has had time to generate more domestic technology since 1917 than the Soviet Union. In addition, North American and Western European technology has flowed to Eastern Europe since the Second World War and has thus become indirectly available to the Soviet Union.

FIVE

The Transfer of Western Technology

The New Economic Policy: the 1920s

Three years after the October Revolution, when the Russian economy lay prostrate in the wake of the civil war, Lenin proclaimed his New Economic Policy, based on the revival of small-scale private enterprise in agriculture and industry. As part of this tactical move to introduce a temporary measure of economic and trade liberalisation, in order to put Russia's economy back on its feet, he invited Western firms back to Moscow and asked them to establish concessions. The attraction of this policy was that it would enable foreign entrepreneurs to establish business operations in the Soviet Union without gaining property rights.

Lenin's objective was thus to lure foreign capital and skills to the Soviet Union in order to introduce Western techniques into her dormant post-revolutionary economy. It was also his intention to expropriate the concessions once production was under way. Hence his statement to a meeting of the CPSU in 1920: '. . . concessions do not mean peace with capitalism, but war on a new plane'.[1]

Altogether during this period, some 350 concessions were granted to foreign firms, which flocked to the Soviet Union with their technicians, machinery, and capital. Some of the most famous Western companies were involved: General Electric, Westinghouse, International Harvester, RCA, Alcoa, Singer, Du Pont, Ford, and Standard Oil from the United States; Krupp, Thyssens, Otto Wolff, Siemens, the AEG, Junkers, Telefunken and I.G.Farben from Germany; finally, concessions were also established by important English, French, Swedish, Danish and

---

[1] Quoted by Carl Gershman in 'Selling Them the Rope: Business and the Soviets', *Commentary*, Vol. 67, No. 4 (published by the American Jewish Committee), New York, April 1979. Lenin also remarked, in 1920, that 'This is a new sort of war, an economic struggle between two systems, the communist and the capitalist. We shall prove that we are the stronger . . . And as soon as we are strong enough to overthrow capitalism, we shall immediately seize it by the throat.' (Quoted in Werner Keller, *Are The Russians Ten Feet Tall?*, Thames & Hudson, London, 1961, p. 214.)

Austrian companies. Foreign concessions were employed in every sector of the economy except furniture and fittings, and the largest single group of concessions was in raw material development, especially oil. Dr Sutton writes:

'In the Caucasus oil fields—then seen as the key to economic recovery by virtue of the foreign exchange that oil exports would generate—the International Barnsdall Corporation introduced American rotary drilling techniques and pumping technology. By the end of the 1920s 80% of Soviet oil drilling was conducted by the American rotary technique; there had been no rotary drilling at all in Russia at the time of the Revolution.

International Barnsdall also introduced a technical revolution in oil pumping and electrification of oil fields. All refineries were built by foreign corporations, although only one, the Standard Oil lease at Batum, was under a concessionary arrangement—the remainder were built under contract.'[1]

The favourable impact of this flow of Western technology was substantial since Soviet production was almost zero in 1922 but had regained pre-World War I figures by 1928. Dr Sutton's conclusion is that for the period 1917 to 1930:

'Western assistance in various forms was the *single most important factor* first in the sheer survival of the Soviet regime and secondly in industrial progress to pre-revolutionary levels.'[2] (My italics.)

The reversal of Soviet policy

In accordance with original Leninist objectives, all foreign concessions granted at the beginning of the 'twenties were expropriated by the early 'thirties. By 1933, none were left, although numerous companies had signed contracts covering 30 to 50 years. As Carl Gershman has written:

'Some of the concessions were closed down by force, but the more common methods were punitive taxation, breach of contract, legal harassment, and disruptions by workers.
The largest concession of all, the British mining company, Lena Goldfields Ltd., had assembled its technicians, invested almost $80 million in equipment, and completed its surveys when it was attacked as a "weed in the socialist system". The OGPU[3] raided its units, threw out many of its personnel, and jailed several of its leading technicians on charges of "industrial espionage".'[4]

---

[1] Sutton, *op. cit.*, Vol. 3, p. 411.

[2] *Ibid.*, p. 412.

[3] The title then given to the Soviet secret police, today's KGB.

[4] Gershman, *op. cit.*, p. 37; also Werner Keller, *op. cit.*, pp. 217-18, 222.

Only a handful were compensated. Firms which had already lost their holdings in 1917 suffered the unpleasant experience of being expropriated twice.

1930-1945

The liquidation of foreign concessions did not, remarkably, signal the end of Western business involvement. Rather it marked the beginning of the most substantial transfer of Western technology yet undertaken, in the form of American assistance to the first Five Year Plan (1928-33).

The plan was largely implemented by American managers and engineers. Stalin himself told the President of the US Chamber of Commerce, in 1944,[1] that two-thirds of the large industrial projects in the Soviet Union had been built with American assistance. Indeed, the general design and construction of the gigantic plants built between 1929 and 1933, plus much of their equipment, was provided by the Detroit firm, Albert Kahn Inc., then generally regarded as the most prominent industrial architects in the USA[2] (for example, it built Ford's River Rouge factory). The construction of the Magnitogorsk steelworks, the largest in the world, was carried out by the Arthur G. Mckee Company of Cleveland. General Electric built and installed the massive generators at the Dniepr and further designed the Kharkov turbine works with a manufacturing capacity two and a half times its own central plant at Schenectady. The Austin Company constructed the huge car plant at Gorki (known as 'the Detroit of the USSR'). Russia's other car plants, at Moscow and Yaroslavl, were built respectively by the A. J. Brandt Company of Detroit and the Herculese Motor Corporation of Canton, Ohio. Finally, Austin's John Calder supervised the construction of Europe's largest tractor plant at Stalingrad.[3]

Soviet sources indicate that as well as receiving complete industrial plants in this period, the Soviet Union also imported 300,000 high-quality foreign machine-tools between 1929 and 1940.[4]

---

[1] Gershman, *ibid.,* p. 37; also Alexander Solzhenitsyn's speech to the AFL-CIO (the American equivalent of the TUC), Washington DC, 30 June 1975, reprinted as *Solzhenitsyn: The Voice of Freedom*, American Federation of Labour and Congress of Industrial Organisations, Publication No. 152, Washington DC, p. 5.

[2] Sutton, Vol. 3, p. 143.

[3] Further details are in *Commentary*, December 1979.

[4] Sutton, Vol. 3, p. 413.

Table 5:
Major Categories of Lend-Lease Supply to the Soviet Union

Category	Quantity shipped
Aircraft and equipment	14,018 units
Vehicles (including tanks and trucks)	466,968 units
Explosives	325,784 short tons
Naval and marine equipment	5,367,000 gross registered tons of shipping, and 7,617 marine engines
Foodstuffs	4,291,012 short tons
Industrial machinery and equipment	$1,095 million
Materials and metal products	2,589,776 short tons of steel, 781,663 short tons of non-ferrous metals, 1,018,855 miles of wire, 2,159,336 short tons of petroleum, 820,422 short tons of chemicals

Source: US Department of State, *Report on War Aid Furnished by the United States to the USSR*, Office of Foreign Liquidation, Washington DC, 1945, pp. 20-28.

Lend-Lease during World War II

The transfer of Western technology, already considerable during the 1930s, received an added fillip after the German attack in 1941. Under Lend-Lease, the Soviets received $11 billion-worth of military and non-military goods from the United States between 1941 and 1946. Table 5 shows the major categories of supplies and the approximate amounts shipped between June 1941 and September 1945.

What is significant about Lend-Lease is that, together with its associated and supplementary post-war programmes, it injected about $1·25 billion-worth[1] of the latest American industrial equipment into the Soviet economy. It included machines and technologies generally in advance of Soviet wartime capabilities, and so was of significant value to the economic development of the USSR.

Post-war plunder: an additional source of new technology

Apart from Lend-Lease, the Soviet Union derived technological benefit from her removal of over $10 billion-worth (at 1938 prices) of equipment from occupied areas in the aftermath of the

---

[1] This figure *excludes* the value of foodstuffs, semi-fabricated materials, industrial supplies, and vehicles of indirect benefit.

war.[1] The Russians acquired, for example, 41 per cent of Germany's 1943 industrial capacity as a result of the removal of several thousand plants from the Soviet zone. In addition they were allowed to remove 25 per cent of all the plants to be found in the Western Allied zones.[2] Thus by the end of 1946 about 95 per cent of the plants being dismantled in the US zone were for the USSR—including the aircraft plants of Daimler-Benz, ball-bearing facilities, and several munition plants. Further booty consisted of the famous Karl Zeiss factory at Jena which manu-factured precision optical instruments, as well as the Opel car works at Brandenburg. Altogether, at least two-thirds of Germany's aircraft industry, probably two-thirds of her electrical industry, and the major part of her rocket production industry were transferred to the Soviet Union.[3] The rocket works, which included the huge underground V-2 plant at Nordhausen, laid the foundation of the Soviet 'Sputnik' programme.

Germany was not the only country looted. By the spring of 1946 the Soviets had also dismantled and removed $895 million-worth of industrial equipment from Manchuria.[4] A further $400 million of equipment was taken from the Soviet zone in Austria. Peace treaties with Finland and Rumania resulted in the transfer of $600 million of equipment.[5]

Summary: the impact by 1945

By 1945 the Soviet Union's industrial structure consisted mainly of large units (mostly built by foreign companies at the beginning of the 1930s) producing standardised models copied from foreign designs and manufactured with foreign equipment. Although the Soviets no longer required (as a general rule) foreign engineers for most of the years 1930-45, they still required foreign designs, foreign machines and complete foreign plants in new technical areas. By 1945

'... the Soviet Union had "caught up" at least twice; once in the 1930s (it could also be argued that the assistance of the 1920s constituted the first catching-up) with the construction of the first Five Year Plan by foreign companies, and again in 1945 as a result of the massive flow of Western technology under Lend-Lease.

---

[1] Sutton, Vol. 3, p. 39.   [2] *Ibid.*, p. 26.   [3] *Ibid.*, p. 414.

[4] Edwin Pauley, *Report on Japanese Assets in Manchuria to the President of the United States,* Washington DC, July 1946.

[5] F. Nemschak, *Ten Years of Austrian Economic Development, 1945-1955,* Association of Austrian Industrialists, Vienna, 1955, p. 8; Bartell C. Jensen, *The Impact of Reparations on the Post-War Finnish Economy,* Richard D. Irwin, Homewood, Illinois, 1966; Sutton, Vol. 3, pp. 32-38.

While the technical skills demonstrated by the Tsarist craftsmen had not quite been achieved [Tsarist-era technology was of a higher standard than is generally believed: it had achieved the capability to produce aircraft, calculating machines, and locomotives], it may be said that in 1945 the nucleus of a skilled engineering force was once again available in Russia—for the first time since the Revolution.'[1]

The post-war transfer of Western technology: 1945-65

In the late 1950s the Soviet leaders turned their attention to remedying their deficiencies in the chemical, computer, shipbuilding and consumer industries. They embarked upon a vast complete-plant purchasing programme. They bought from Western Europe[2] at least 50 complete chemical plants between 1959 and 1963, to manufacture chemicals not previously produced in the USSR. Similarly, a gigantic ship-purchasing programme was organised so that by 1967 two-thirds of the Soviet merchant fleet had been built in the West.[3]

Soviet acquisition of computers and similar advanced technologies met with more difficulty up to 1965. This no doubt partly explained the state of technological backwardness of which Academician Sakharov, the 'father of the Soviet hydrogen bomb', complained in 1969. In a letter to the Soviet party leadership he warned:

'A second Industrial Revolution has begun and today, at the beginning of the seventies, we can see that not only have we not overtaken America, but we are falling behind her ever further . . . Our total computer capacity is *hundreds of times smaller* than that of the USA, and as for the utilisation of computers in the economy, the gap is too great to be calculated. We are, quite simply, living in a different epoch.'[4] (My italics.)

In more recent years, from the end of the 'sixties onwards, the Soviet Union has been able to purchase high-grade Western computers. During the early 'seventies, for instance, an American company, Control Data Corporation, signed a 10-year agreement with the Soviet Ministry of Science and Technology which included a plan for the joint development of a new super computer. A spokesman for the Control Data Corporation admitted that the Soviets thereby gained 15 years in research and development, and at the cost of spending only $3 million over three years.[5]

---

[1] Sutton, Vol. 3, p. 414.

[2] The countries involved included Britain, Belgium, France, Austria, Italy and West Germany.

[3] Sutton, Vol. 3, p. 415.

[4] Quoted by Professor Tibor Szamuely, Postscript to *Half-Marx, op. cit.*

[5] Gershman, *op. cit.*, p. 39.

Table 6:
United Kingdom Deliveries to the Soviet Union under the 1947 Trade Agreement

	Schedule I			Schedule II	
Item No.	Quantity	Description	Item No.	Quantity	Description
1	1,100	Narrow gauge locomotives 750-mm	1	£150,000 value	Scientific and laboratory apparatus
2	2,400	Flat trucks 750-mm	2	4	Pile drivers mounted on pontoons
3	2,400	Winches (2 & 3 drums)	3	4 sets	Winding gear
4	210	Excavators	4	1	Electro dredger
5	54	Caterpillar loading cranes	5	18	Ball mills for copper ore grinding
6	250	Auto timber carriers	6	8	Ball mills for grinding apatite
7	14	Tugs	7	3	Rod mills for grinding ores
8	4	Dredgers	8	8	Spiral-type classifiers
9	200	Locomobiles	9	2	Gyratory crushers
10	150	Mobile diesel electric generators, 50 kw	10	3	Railway steam cranes
11	24	Steam power turbine stations 500 kw	11	48	154-kv Voltage transformers
12	£1,050,000 value	Plywood equipment	12	6	Complete distributing sets
13	£400,000 value	Timber mill equipment	13	45	Isolating switches (154 kv)
			14	10	Oil purifying apparatus
			15	300	100-kw electric motors

Source: Great Britain, Soviet Union No. 1 (1948), Cmd, 7297, HMSO, London, 1948.

The transfer of British technology: 1947-69

A substantial amount of British technology has been transferred to the Soviet Union under a number of trade agreements. In 1947 the UK agreed to the immediate export of 35,000 long tons of light rails (complete with fishplates, nuts and bolts) to the USSR, in exchange for Soviet barley, maize and oats. In the longer term, the UK further agreed to export oil-well tubes, tinplate, and the materials listed under Schedules I and II in Table 6, in exchange for supplies of Soviet wheat, pulses, pit props, cellulose and canned goods.

Under a five-year trade agreement in 1959, Britain was to export (in exchange for raw materials) equipment for the Soviet chemical industry and for the pulp and paper industry; forging, stamping and casting equipment; metalworking machine-tools; equipment for the electro-technical and cable industry and for the automation of production processes; compression and refrigeration equipment; and equipment for sugar beet factories, the building industry and light industry.[1]

The 1959 agreement was extended for another five years in 1964, while the quotas for the period 1959-69 ensured a continuing supply of British technology to the USSR. Thus in that decade, the Soviet Union was able to import machine-tools, earth-moving, mechanical handling, mining, gas and arc welding, chemical, refrigeration and compressor equipment, and, finally, a wide range of scientific and optical instruments.[2]

The revealing nature of Soviet exports

The technological inferiority of the Soviet economy has reflected itself in the Soviet Union's post-war export trade. In the late 1960s (and similarly today) Soviet exports consisted largely of raw materials and semi-manufactured goods like chrome, manganese, pig iron, glass blocks, furs and foodstuffs. When manufactured goods were exported they were usually machine-tools and vehicles, based on Western designs and exported to under-developed countries. Even ailing Soviet foreign aid projects have been rescued from failure by foreign equipment, as with the Aswan Dam where British and Swedish equipment was employed.

The Soviets have, it is true, made strenuous efforts to export manufactures to advanced Western markets—for example, watches, cars and tractors. Technical breakdowns of these goods, however, have typically revealed that they are either of Western origin, or else contain Western components where the products have been assembled in the West.[3]

---

[1] United Nations, *Treaty Series,* Vol. 374, Nos. 5,323- 5,350, New York, 1960, p. 308.

[2] A complete statement of the quotas and the 1959 agreement is in Peter Zentner, *East-West Trade: A Practical Guide to Selling in Eastern Europe,* Max Parrish, London, 1967, pp. 152-57.

[3] Sutton, Vol. 3, p. 415.

The continuing lack of Soviet innovation in the early 1970s

Although in an earlier period of Soviet development some indigenous Soviet innovation took place (Table 3, p. 24), the post-
war years have seen a move back towards the use of Western
technology even there. SK-B, a Russian-developed synthetic
rubber, has been increasingly replaced by Western synthetic
rubbers. There has been renewed research into developing the
techniques of rotary drilling, proved necessary in the wake of the
inefficiency resulting from the use of the Soviet turbodrill. The
Russian boiler has sometimes been abandoned in favour of
Western designs. The evidence therefore suggests that the Soviet
economy was *technically* still an imperfect copy of its Western
counterparts as late as 1970.[1]

Today, at the beginning of the 1980s, it seems that this backwardness has not materially altered. This verdict has been recently
confirmed by the controversial sale by Dresser Industries (USA) of
a $144 million turnkey plant for the manufacture of deep-well
drilling equipment to produce 100,000 high-quality oil-drilling
bits per year, equipment extremely difficult to buy outside the
United States because other countries have not yet mastered the
technology. The Soviet Union is having to import this technology
in order to develop major new oil reserves since, on present trends,
she will become a net importer of oil by the mid-1980s.

---

[1] *Ibid.*, p. 415.

SIX

The Ultimate Role of Western Technology in the Soviet System: Conclusions

1. Substitute for indigenous innovation

Domestic innovation is the missing ingredient in the Soviet economic system. Central planning and collectivist monopoly are the key organisational factors responsible for this inherent deficiency (pp. 21-22). The principal rôle of Western technological transfers has thus been to act as a vital substitute for the self-generating innovation without which no economy can grow and prosper beyond a primitive level. Imported technology has provided the USSR with the missing dynamic element of technical progress.

The process has followed a fairly standard sequence:

'First, at an early stage in a sector's development the productive units themselves are imported, i.e. the machines, the boilers, the production lines. This is followed by a second stage, that of duplication or copying of the most useful of the imported units, according to a standardised design. Long runs of standard units without model change achieve the favourable growth rates that characterise selected sectors of the Soviet economy.
In certain sectors this may be followed by a third stage—adaptive innovation, i.e. scaling-up . . . Such scaling-up, however, cannot be applied in all sectors or in all basic technologies within a sector.'[1]

As well as providing a source of technical modernisation, imported Western technology releases domestic resources for military uses by saving the Soviet Union large sums in research and development costs. It also provides more 'performance flexibility' because a standardised design is suitable for only a limited range of end-uses, such as the marine boilers installed in Soviet ships between 1945 and 1960. Because all Soviet-made marine boilers are of one size and model, flexibility for various requirements has been achieved through the import of boilers with non-standard characteristics. Finally, and not least important, technological transfers put engineering skill into the Soviet economy by being

---

[1] Sutton, Vol. 3, pp. 402-403.

embodied in the foreign construction of large production units—those beyond available Soviet skills but not necessarily requiring new technology.

2. Helps fulfil planning objectives

The Soviets have generally looked to imported technology to enable them to achieve planned increases in output, when these have not been achievable by duplication or by 'scaling-up' innovation. Processes acquired in this way have generally been those whose development abroad required large investments in capital and skill.

This tactic becomes clear from the composition of Soviet imports. Between 1946 and 1966 total imports increased 10-fold, from 692 million roubles in 1946 to 7,122 million roubles in 1966. The import of machinery and equipment remained consistently at one-third of the total—197 million roubles in 1946, 2,308 million roubles in 1966. Analysis of the components of this import trade reveals that planning objectives and directives have reflected themselves in significant increases in imports in the affected sectors, as in both the chemical and shipbuilding industries.

Khrushchev's call, in 1957, for a large increase in Soviet chemical production was accompanied by an immediate increase in imports of chemical equipment. Thus chemical imports increased 10-fold between 1957 and 1966, from 22 million roubles to just over 200 million roubles.

Soviet import figures have also reflected internal shortages, especially in agriculture. As a result of the agricultural problems of the early 1960s, for example, there were large imports of foreign wheat, fertilizers and agricultural equipment. These, in total, rose from 14 million roubles in 1961 to 62 million roubles in 1966.

Table 7 provides a detailed picture of the pattern of Soviet imports over this period. Dr Sutton calculates that Soviet plans for the chemical, synthetic fibre, rubber, automobile and merchant marine industries could not have been fulfilled even by 10 per cent if the Soviets had been solely reliant on domestic abilities and resources during these years.

Some might argue that Soviet imports of Western technology reflect a conscious reliance on the international division of labour rather than an attempt to compensate for technological backwardness, particularly since other countries (e.g. Japan) also import (or have imported) technology. The sheer scale of Soviet dependence on Western technology over at least half a century, plus the inherent institutional/collectivist obstacles to native Soviet innovation, suggest otherwise. Furthermore, unlike the

Table 7:
Soviet Imports by Soviet Transport Category,
1946 to 1966

	Total imports (million roubles)	Machines & equipment (Groups 10-19)	Ships & equipment (Group 192)	Chemical industry equipment (Group 150)	Agricultural equipment & fertilisers (Groups 181, 342)
1946	692·0	197·4	5·6	3·9	0·1
1947	670·3	119·1	3·9	1·5	0·2
1948	1,106·6	99·0	5·4	0·9	0·1
1949	1,340·3	193·4	23·6	1·9	1·7
1950	1,310·3	281·7	25·8	1·7	6·2
1951	1,791·7	372·0	33·9	6·4	0·4
1952	2,255·5	486·2	71·6	9·3	0·2
1953	2,492·1	684·8	106·7	18·3	0·3
1954	2,863·6	875·4	201·7	23·0	0·5
1955	2,754·5	832·8	237·5	22·1	6·4
1956	3,251·4	805·8	273·8	19·3	6·1
1957	3,544·0	846·4	215·5	22·1	13·0
1958	3,914·6	958·1	214·7	45·5	10·7
1959	4,565·9	1,216·7	271·9	103·4	9·7
1960	5,065·6	1,507·7	340·4	167·0	8·6
1961	5,344·9	1,561·0	203·1	171·0	14·1
1962	5,809·9	2,020·6	332·9	141·8	24·8
1963	6,352·9	2,219·4	366·1	190·2	31·2
1964	6,962·9	2,398·5	483·9	186·4	53·1
1965	7,252·5	2,423·5	489·7	187·4	54·4
1966	7,121·6	2,308·4	493·7	208·0	62·8

Source: Vneshniaia torgovlia SSR: Statisticheskii sbornik, 1918-1966, Moscow, 1967, quoted in Sutton, op. cit., Vol. 3, p. 407.

Soviet Union, Western countries generate a substantial measure of domestic innovation even though they may still import technology ftom outside (like Britain). If the importation of Western technology was not a reflection of technological backwardness, official Soviet writing would not be so coy about admitting the rôle of Western technology in Soviet economic development (p. 30).

In the shipping industry, the irreplaceability of imports is graphically demonstrated by Tables 8 and 9. The foreign suppliers of hulls and engines for the Soviet tanker fleet have included Japan, Italy, Finland, Denmark, Sweden, Holland, Yugoslavia, Poland, Bulgaria and East Germany.

Table 8:
Foreign Construction of Marine Diesel Engines
for the Soviet Tanker Fleet, 1951-July 1967

	Total installed in Soviet tankers	Foreign	Percentage foreign-built
	number		%
1951	2	1	50
1952	7	6	86
1953	16	13	81
1954	14	4	28
1955	17	8	47
1956	25	14	56
1957	33	19	58
1958	17	9	53
1959	16	4	25
1960	15	3	20
1961	11	6	54
1962	21	18	86
1963	16	11	68
1964	22	19	86
1965	21	18	86
1966	22	12	55
1967	7	4	57
Totals	281	169	60 percent average

Source: Calculated from Registr Soyuza SSR, *Registrovaya kniga morskikh sudov soyuza SSR 1964-1965*, Moscow, 1966; quoted in Sutton, Vol. 3, p. 298.

By July 1967 about two-thirds of the Soviet tanker fleet had been built outside the Soviet Union, and the foreign-built segment included almost all tankers in excess of 13,000 tons. Two-thirds of the smaller tankers were built abroad rather than in the Soviet Union, including those for coastal use and for use in the Caspian Sea. Even some of the tankers built in the Soviet Union had engines manufactured abroad, imported into the USSR, and then installed in hulls built in Soviet yards.

3. Critical influence on Soviet growth rates
Central planning, whatever its other weaknesses, is able to realise substantial rates of growth in a *few* sectors through the planned diversion of efforts and resources into them (pp. 29-30). Russian

Table 9:
Construction of the Soviet Tanker Fleet, 1951 to 1967

	Hull and engine built in USSR tons	Hull and/or engine built outside USSR tons	Total added to tanker fleet tons	Percentage built outside USSR %
1951	8,229	1,113	9,342	11·9
1952	8,229	14,618	22,847	65·0
1953	24,687	16,570	41,257	40·1
1954	77,798	4,468	82,266	5·4
1955	65,077	20,721	85,798	24·1
1956	60,337	46,820	107,157	43·7
1957	59,532	54,109	113,641	47·6
1958	18,556	35,502	54,058	65·7
1959	90,066	24,663	114,729	21·5
1960	93,707	105,827	199,534	53·0
1961	31,074	56,397	87,471	64·5
1962	42,510	178,879	221,389	80·8
1963	87,693	179,055	266,748	67·1
1964	164,205	328,265	492,470	66·6
1965	132,872	242,201	375,073	64·6
1966	234,235	145,857	380,092	38·4
1967	—	41,833	41,833	100·0
Totals	1,198,807	1,496,898	2,695,705	55·6 percent average

Source: Calculated from Registr Soyuza SSR, *Registrovaya kniga morskikh sudov soyuza SSR 1964-1965*, Moscow, 1966; quoted in Sutton, Vol. 3, p. 297.

pig-iron production, for example, rose from 4·2 million tons in 1913 to 70·3 million tons in 1966, and steel production increased from 4·3 million tons in 1913 to 96·9 million tons in 1966. In these (and other) sectors where exceptional rates of growth have been experienced, there has usually been a significant acquisition of Western technology at the start of the rise in growth. Planned increments in Soviet production have been consciously achieved by the purchase of advanced high productivity industrial units in the West. This policy strongly suggests that the Soviet system could not have achieved high rates of growth in any single sector without external injections of technology and capacity.

Even the iron and steel industry, which has come closest to showing indigenous technical progress, first had to absorb

Western technology and then 'scale-up' in order to provide the increases in pig-iron and raw steel output.

A general conclusion about the performance of centrally planned economies is that they can prosper only if there are market-oriented economies willing to provide them with the necessary technical services and productive units. (This process is currently repeating itself in the Far East, where Communist China is beginning to import technology from Britain, the United States and Japan.) A world of centrally-planned systems based on the Soviet model, or a single centrally-planned world system, could not progress. It would choke on technical inertia.

This conclusion runs parallel to the one reached earlier (pp. 19-20) about the need of Iron Curtain planners to base their internal pricing on the data provided by existing world market prices. It reinforces the view that a wholly communist world would not be economically viable.

4. Western technology and the Soviet 'military complex'

During a large part of its existence, the Soviet régime has received substantial direct military aid: from Germany before 1930[1] and from the United States after 1941 under Lend-Lease. What is being discussed here is the rôle Western *civilian* technology has played both in promoting Soviet military programmes and releasing internal resources for military uses.

Much modern technology has both military and civilian uses. Air traffic control systems can be employed for air defence and for vectoring fighter aircraft. Similarly, the semi-conductor technology used in computers can be applied to missile guidance systems, and the technology employed in the manufacture of wide-body aircraft and high-bypass turbofan jet engines can be used in the production of military aircraft. Consequently it is likely that a significant proportion of imported Western technology has contributed indirectly to the construction of the Soviet military machine.

American computer technology has contributed to Soviet advances in strategic weaponry while many Western-built Soviet factories are easily convertible to military production. Thus a senior American official[2] has recently made the controversial claim that

---

[1] A detailed account of how the Germans (Junkers) built up the Soviet aircraft industry during this period is in Werner Keller, *op. cit.*, pp. 219-222. Also Sutton, Vol. 1: *1917-1930*.

[2] Lawrence J. Brady, deputy director of the US Commerce Department's Office of Export Administration, in testimony to the US House Armed Services Committee, May 1979.

the giant Kama River truck factory in Siberia, built with $500 million-worth of American designs and equipment in 1971, is being employed for military purposes. The plant is apparently producing transport and scout vehicles, armoured personnel carriers, assault vehicles and battle tank engines for the Soviet armed forces.[1] Whether or not this information is correct, the Kama River factory (like many others) has a military potential. It is, therefore, difficult to draw a distinction between military and civilian goods. Hence this conclusion, in 1977, from the former Chairman of the American Defence Science Board Task Force on the Export of US Technology:

'the transfer [to the USSR] of militarily significant technology has been of major proportions, the full consequences of which will become evident over the next five years.'[2]

Ultimately the most important contribution of Western technology to Soviet military development has been to provide the Soviet armed forces with the necessary industrial support system. Not only have the USSR's domestic resources been freed for military purposes;[3] her industrial base has been updated and fortified by foreign assistance. Thus the Soviet 'military-industrial complex'[4] has been able to incorporate the latest Western manufacturing techniques.

It was undoubtedly with these considerations in mind that President Leonid Brezhnev observed in 1972:

'Scientific-technical progress has now become one of the main bridge-heads of the historical struggle of the two systems'.[5]

---

[1] Peter C. Stuart, 'Will US back personnel who blow the whistle?', *Christian Science Monitor*, 26 November 1979, p. 6.

[2] Gershman, *op. cit.*, p. 42.

[3] Although completely accurate estimates are hard to come by, most experts agree that between 12 and 25 per cent of the Soviet Union's GNP is devoted to military purposes (Brian Crozier, *Strategy of Survival*, Temple Smith, 1978, p. 41). CIA estimates indicate that Soviet military spending exceeds that of the United States by approximately 40 per cent in absolute terms. The Soviet Union spends *twice* as much as the USA on the acquisition of arms and on military research and development, and *three* times as much on strategic arms. (Fred Iklé, 'Arms Control and National Defense', in Peter Duignan and Alvin Rabushka (eds.), *The United States in the 1980s*, The Hoover Institution, Stanford, California, 1980.)

[4] A term supposedly coined by the late President Eisenhower.

[5] Gershman, *op. cit.*, p. 45.

SEVEN

East-West Trade and the Political Economy of Technological Transfers

Trade will 'civilise the Bolsheviks': the orthodox view

The notion that trade encourages peace and is the ally of personal freedom was the traditional conviction of 19th-century liberalism. More economic interdependence between nations, other things being equal, tends to foster mutual co-operation and understanding as well as to raise the potential economic cost of war. Consequently the belief in the essentially civilising rôle of international commerce has always had respectable advocates—especially in the case of East-West trade.

In 1922, for example, Lloyd George (then Prime Minister) declared that trade with Russia 'will bring an end to the ferocity, the rapine, and the crudity of Bolshevism surer than any other method'. This view was not shared by Winston Churchill in 1924. In a speech at Edinburgh on 25 September, Churchill attacked Ramsay MacDonald's proposed Anglo-Soviet Treaty:

> 'I object to subsidising tyranny. Judged by every standard which history has applied to Governments, the Soviet Government of Russia is one of the worst tyrannies that has ever existed in the world'.[1]

In 1918 Lloyd George's view had been stated by Edwin Gay, a member of the US War Trade Board and former Dean of Harvard Business School. The War Trade Board's official minutes recorded him as saying:

> '. . . it was doubtful whether the policy of blockade and economic isolation of those portions of Russia . . . under Bolshevik control [during the civil war between "Reds" and "Whites"] was the best policy for bringing about the establishment of a stable and proper Government in Russia. Mr Gay suggested to the Board that if the people in the Bolshevik sections of Russia were given the opportunity to enjoy improved economic conditions, they would themselves bring about the establishment of a moderate and stable social order.'[2]

---

[1] Quoted by Martin Gilbert in *Winston Churchill*, Vol. V: *1922-39*, Heinemann, London, 1976, p. 48.

[2] Vol. 5, 5 December 1918, pp. 43-44.

Today this view remains influential even in the wake of the Soviet invasion of Afghanistan. Thus despite former President Carter's clampdown on the export of American computer technology to the Soviet Union, people in high places advocate Soviet-Western trade in the supposed interests of peace.[1] Carter's measures, imposed on 18 March 1980, were expected to produce 'a cut of up to 70 per cent in the $200 million (£91 million) high technology exports "that can be used by the Soviet Union to advance its military capability" '.[2] However, according to Lawrence J. Brady, who served for more than five years in the US Department of Commerce, Carter's technology embargo was 'a gimmick' since it applied to '6 or 7 per cent of what we export to the Soviet Union. 93 per cent of what we export to the Soviets in terms of manufactured goods is not embargoed at the moment.'[3]

Trade is profitable to the Western businessman

The political case advanced in favour of trade with the Soviet Union is supported by substantial business interests anxious to exploit the possibilities of opening up the Soviet market to Western goods and skills. Thus the former President of the US-USSR Trade and Economic Council, Harold B. Scott, argues:

'[the USSR] will one day be the largest market in the world. The systems put in place there now will determine the patterns of trade. Now is the time when it is crucially important to put our technology there.'[4]

The apparent profitability of trade with the USSR is still generally insisted upon although the Soviets are reputed to be hard bargainers and to indulge in numerous unethical commercial practices. Firms have continued to make deals despite the Soviet theft of blueprints and specifications, and their duplication of these firms' equipment without permission or the payment of royalties.[5]

Western businessmen's perception of the advantages of dealing with the USSR have also survived the adverse consequences

---

[1] As *The Times* reported on 22 January 1980, Mr Guido Brunner, the EEC Commissioner for Energy, condemned the use of economic sanctions against the Soviet Union as 'doomed to failure . . . The Soviet Union can only be "conquered" by involvement in a web of economic ties with the rest of the world'.

[2] *Daily Telegraph* report, 19 March 1980.

[3] Interview in *Human Events*, Vol. XXX, No. 9, Washington DC, 1 March 1980.

[4] Gershman, *op. cit.*, p. 40.

[5] Sutton, Vol. 2: *1930-45*, pp. 263-67.

flowing from the state monopoly of Soviet foreign trade. As the sole buyer from numerous sellers (competing American, European and Japanese firms), the Soviet Government enjoys unequal bargaining power which can be employed to cut prices and to secure other benefits such as technical data and licences, extensive training of Soviet personnel, and long-term arrangements for the continuous supply of new technology. *Large* firms, such as General Electric, Imperial Chemical Industries, and Union Carbide, are often able to obtain more equitable treatment because they are likely to receive the backing of their governments in difficult bargaining. Furthermore the Soviets are wary of pushing their luck where the available sources of desirable new technologies are relatively few.

The voluntary participation of profit-seeking Western businessmen in East-West trade implies that it is profitable, despite the vagaries of Soviet behaviour. The real question is the extent to which the economic benefits are counterbalanced by the long-term *political* consequences.

Western ignorance of technological transfers to the USSR

Favourable attitudes towards Western-Soviet trade have tended to coincide with widespread ignorance about the extent of technological transfers. Not surprisingly, this ignorance has in turn encouraged the error that imported Western technology has played only a minor rôle in Soviet economic development. Soviet achievements have therefore been made to look far more impressive than they are. This error has been common among officials and the public since the war, though less so today.

In 1961, for instance, the US Information Agency conducted a survey[1] of European opinion on the relative success of American and Soviet scientific and technical achievements. More Western Europeans believed the Soviet Union was technically ahead of the United States than *vice-versa*. This opinion varied from country to country. In Britain, 59 per cent thought the Soviet Union was ahead as opposed to 21 per cent favouring the United States; in West Germany half the respondents put the USA ahead of the USSR.

In official circles, the US State Department has consistently

---

[1] Leo P. Crespi, 'The Image of US Versus Soviet Science in Western European Public Opinion', in R. L. Merrit and D. J. Puchala (eds.), *Western European Perspectives on International Affairs: Public Opinion Studies and Evaluations,* Praeger, New York, 1967.

argued, since 1918, that Soviet industrial development has had little connection with Western technology, including trade and other mechanisms of technological transfer. A prominent example of the State Department's thinking is an extract from its *Battle Act Report: 1963,* submitted to Congress:

'[Trade with the West has made an] obviously limited contribution to Soviet economic and industrial growth.'[1]

The report asserted that denial of trade would not affect basic Soviet military capability and went on to explain why the 1963 Battle Act embargo (prohibiting the export of certain strategic materials to the Soviet Union) was not as extensive as its predecessors in the 1950s:

'the inevitable process of industrial and economic growth during those twelve years has meant that the Soviets have developed their own productive capability in many of the areas where a restraining impact was necessary and possible ten years ago.'

These comments were made at a time when the Soviets were midway through the purchase of complete industrial sectors from the West, such as concentrated fertilizers, synthetic rubbers and fibres, engines, computers, electric locomotives and cars, for Soviet industrial sectors that were either non-existent or extremely backward in 1963.[2]

Official illusions about the nature and extent of Soviet economic achievements have been accompanied down the years by a multitude of unofficial but erroneous predictions that the Soviet Union was winning (or would win) the economic race with the West. Isaac Deutscher's *The Great Contest* (1959) was a prominent example; so was Michael Shanks's best-seller of the early 1960s, *The Stagnant Society.*[3]

Western technology and the 'contradictions of communism'

In the end, the most valuable function of Western technology in the Soviet system is that it helps resolve what can be described as the inner contradiction of Soviet Communism: the conflict between the political and economic objectives of the Soviet rulers.

---

[1] *Battle Act Report 1963*, Washington DC, 1963, p. 8.

[2] Sutton, Vol. 3, p. xxviii.

[3] Penguin Books, 1961 (revised Edn. 1972).

Given the essential unworkability of a centrally planned collectivist economy, the Soviets face considerable pressures to liberalise their economic system in the interests of innovation, efficiency and balanced growth (to avoid bottlenecks). On the other hand, the Soviet system is a totalitarian one whose leaders are determined to preserve their existing monopoly of power.[1] Economic liberalisation may thus remain a desirable policy for the purpose of domestic industrial regeneration, but it also has the disadvantage of diffusing power and encouraging financial autonomy. Furthermore, it tends to trigger off a chain reaction of additional demands for *political* liberalisation, which cannot be contained within the political structure of the Soviet State once this liberalisation process has overstepped narrow limits.

The ensuing dilemma facing the rulers of the USSR is therefore an exceptionally acute one: either they allow their country to become increasingly poor and backward relative to the West, *or* they introduce liberal reforms that will eventually destroy them politically. The dilemma is especially painful given their realisation that the military and police power upon which their political supremacy rests must be adequately sustained by a modern industrial base. The Soviet leaders are thus constantly obliged to look for ways of obtaining new technology *without* setting in motion a politically dangerous transformation of Soviet society.

Such a contradictory strategy would be unrealisable were it not that the import of Western technology saves the Soviet leadership from having to impale itself upon the horns of this dilemma. For most of the last half century, the Soviet Union has been able both to buy Western technology and keep Western ideas and influence at bay. Today this policy continues with the periodic jamming of the BBC World Service, the Voice of America and other foreign radio stations.

The extent to which the Soviets prevent free cultural contacts

---

[1] The Communist Party's monopoly of power is safeguarded and enforced by the secret police (the KGB), whose agents and outside informers penetrate all Soviet institutions, from the armed forces and the Union of Writers to the CPSU itself. The KGB employs half a million men who include: 90,000 staff officers (spies) spread throughout the world, 300,000 border guards equipped with the latest weaponry (including naval forces), and 100,000 special troops, building guards, and clerical workers. The overwhelming majority of KGB personnel, as these figure indicate, are engaged in internal repression as opposed to espionage abroad. The KGB is reinforced by 70,000 full-time censors employed throughout the USSR by *Glavlit*. (John Barron, *The KGB: The Secret Work of Soviet Secret Agents*, Bantam Books, 1976, especially Chs. 3 and 5.)

with the West while helping themselves to Western products and processes is illustrated by an incident related by Carl Gershman:

'To realise how far the Soviet authorities are willing to go to prevent any contacts from taking place outside of very tightly controlled official channels, one need only think of the confiscation of follow-up cards passed out at a seminar in Moscow conducted by Singer personnel, or the removal of subscription forms from all copies of *Aviation Week and Space Technology* distributed at the Raytheon exhibition.'[1]

Russian dissidents argue for Western restrictions

The argument that imported Western technology lets Soviet Communism off its dialectical hook is strongly echoed in dissident circles. Thus the inherent obstacles to the initiation of reform from the top are emphasised by the late Andrei Amalrik:

'the trouble lies not so much in the fact that . . . the process of liberalisation, instead of being steadily accelerated, is at times palpably slowed down, perverted or turned back, as in the fact that the very nature of the process gives us ground to doubt its ultimate success . . . if such reform liberalisation were carried out to its logical end it would threaten the power of the party machine.'[2]

Solzhenitsyn emphasises the rôle played by technological transfers in rescuing the Russian economy from its inherent deficiencies:

'The Soviet economy has an extremely low level of efficiency . . . It cannot deal with every problem at once: war, space (which is part of the war effort), heavy industry, light industry, and at the same time the necessity to feed its own population. The forces of the entire Soviet economy are concentrated on war . . . everything which is lacking . . . they get from you. So indirectly you are helping them to rearm. You are helping the Soviet police state.'[3]

The rôle of Western technology in reinforcing internal repression within the Soviet Union is emphasised by the exiled Soviet writer, Alexander Ginzburg, reflecting on his treatment by the Soviet authorities:

'The KGB used German machines to record my conversations, high-powered directional microphones and other devices that can pick up sound from the vibrations of a window in my room. The Soviet Union cannot make these things themselves. They don't have the technology. So they buy it from the West. British firms compete to sell Russia computers, and some of these are used, so I've heard from Soviet pilots, to keep MIG fighters in the air.'[4]

---

[1] Gershman, *op. cit.*, p. 41.

[2] Andrei Amalrik, *Will the Soviet Union Survive Until 1984?*, Harper and Row, New York, 1971, pp. 29-30.

[3] Solzhenitsyn, AFL-CIO speech, *op. cit.*, pp. 45-46.

[4] Interview with Lord Bethell, *Sunday Telegraph*, 6 January 1980.

Notwithstanding these eloquent pleas, West Germany has recently chosen to expand her trade with the Soviet Union. On 1 July 1980 the West German Government signed an economic pact with the Soviet Union aimed at encouraging the modernisation of Russian industry, the exploitation of raw materials, and the development of Russian energy resources—including nuclear power stations.[1]

---

[1] A protocol to the agreement listed the kind of equipment West Germany is willing to provide the Soviet Union. It includes factory automation gear, calculators and electronic components, semi-conductor materials, petro-chemical plants, turbine-driven drills, coal gasification equipment and X-ray technology. (*Daily Telegraph* report, 2 July 1980.)

EIGHT

The Implications for Western Policy

Six guidelines for policy-makers

1. No coherent thinking about the desirable policy to adopt towards the USSR can take place in an atmosphere of general ignorance about the nature of Soviet economic development. As long as it continues to be believed (outside a tiny circle of experts) that the Soviet Union has largely industrialised herself by her own efforts, policy-makers will not even begin an intelligent discussion of alternative strategies on the export of Western technology to the East. The first essential is that individuals, governments, academic institutions and the press should inform public opinion of the extent to which the Soviet system has been and continues to be supported by Western market-oriented economies.[1] This task ought not to be too difficult given recent evidence of the continuing failures of Soviet planning. Thus the figures presented to the Supreme Soviet by Mr Nikolai Baibakov, Chairman of the State Planning Committee, indicate that the Soviet Union has fallen seriously behind its targets in the current five-year plan.[2]

---

[1] The argument that, because the West exchanges technology for Soviet raw materials, e.g. oil and timber, the Soviet Union is 'supporting' the West as much as *vice-versa*, overlooks three replies:

   (a) the Soviet Union imports Western technology because she cannot generate sufficient domestic innovation within her communist system. Western countries are not similarly dependent on Soviet raw materials, which can be obtained from other sources.

   (b) the Soviets need Western technology even in order to exploit (and export) some of their raw materials—especially oil (pp.32-33 and p. 40).

   (c) East-West trade is politically asymmetrical because of the vital and one-sided contribution of Western technology to the enhancement of Soviet military power.

[2] The Soviet leader, Mr Brezhnev, in a speech to the plenum of the CPSU's Central Committee, informed it that the country 'was running short of energy, railway transport was in chaos, not enough metal was being produced, meat and milk were scarce, food was poor and such common consumer items as toothpaste, washing powder, needles and thread, and baby nappies were hard to find.

[*footnote continued on page 56*]

2. The nature of trade with totalitarian countries and the degree to which it deviates from the classical model of trade between non-totalitarian states should be reconsidered. Does the traditional assumption of 19th-century liberalism, that trade promotes liberty and peace, apply to East-West trade? Is not the true contrast, to quote a 20th-century liberal economist, that

> 'for monolithic Communism, trade with the West is primarily a political act: for the pluralistic West, it is primarily an opportunity for business and profit'?[1]

If so, trade can no longer be automatically regarded as the friend of liberalisation and genuine *detente*.

3. To what extent can an intelligible distinction be drawn between products and technology in East-West trade, between the item produced and the know-how required to produce it? If such a distinction can be made, as the US Defence Science Board seems to believe, there is a powerful case for trying to deny advanced technology to the Soviets without curtailing trade in consumer goods like jazz records, jeans and foreign tourism. Such a policy might stimulate 'consumerism' within the USSR and make it more difficult for her leaders to ignore the wants of their citizens, whilst preventing (or discouraging) them from devoting such a large proportion of the USSR's resources to military and police purposes.

4. In order to make this policy practicable, there must be a willingness among Western politicians and electorates to accept new legal curbs on East-West trade, designed to halt or reduce the outward flow of sophisticated technology to the Soviet Union.[2] The coercive imposition of restrictions on international trade is

---

'Far too little was being done to raise industrial efficiency and the quality of work, and this had led to bottlenecks and shortages. Vast funds had been invested and the labour force had been increased but the final result was less than it should have been, and less than the country's potential allowed. As a result the economy was suffering from imbalances, shortages and insufficient reserves.' (*The Times*, 29 November 1979.)

[1] Wilhelm Röpke, *A Humane Economy*, Liberty Fund, Indianapolis, 1971, p. 140 (first published by Henry Regnery, Chicago, 1960).

[2] Mrs Thatcher's Government has taken some preliminary steps in this direction in response to the Soviet invasion of Afghanistan. Britain is discontinuing cheap export credit to the Soviet Union and the Government has announced its intention of seeking stricter controls on the transfer of sensitive technology to the USSR, in collaboration with other European countries. At the moment this collaboration is wholly lacking since Britain's European partners are currently competing to fill the gaps in East-West trade created by the partial American embargo.

rightly repugnant to liberal sentiments. Nevertheless it is arguable that such measures are necessary, and in the long-term interests of everyone concerned, if we are to avoid a situation in which Western businessmen fulfil Lenin's prediction that 'when things go very hard for us, we will give a rope to the bourgeoisie, and the bourgeoisie will hang itself'.

5. The relative ineffectiveness of economic sanctions in the past as a political weapon designed to isolate countries and influence their internal affairs is not as relevant here as it might seem. The imposition of sanctions on a country whose economy is market-oriented, e.g. Rhodesia (the best-known recent example), is different in kind from the pursuit of the same policy towards a centrally planned economy like the USSR. A collectivised system is incapable of generating sufficient domestic innovation and attaining the flexibility and efficiency in its use of resources required to 'go it alone' in an inhospitable international environment.

6. In a world where technology is widely diffused, a policy that seeks to deny the Soviet Union (and therefore, necessarily, the satellite countries of Eastern Europe) access to it cannot be water-tight. Yet, as Mr Fred Iklé, the former Director of the US Arms Control and Disarmament Agency, has observed: 'Gradual seepage is one thing. It is quite another matter to expedite the spillage of some of the most advanced and complex technologies'.[1] In short, although the Soviet acquisition of Western technology probably cannot be completely prevented, it can at least be *delayed*. This would help to maintain and perhaps even increase the natural technological superiority of the United States (and her allies) over the Soviet Union and, as a result, the West's 'strategic lead time' in most military technologies. Curbs on technological transfers to the Soviet bloc would thus promote the containment of Soviet expansionism and thereby the cause of peace and freedom.

Conclusion
Whatever the drawbacks, in theory or practice, of this strategy, the risks to the West of doing nothing except perpetuate existing trends are almost certainly greater. Even if politicians, businessmen and voters choose to ignore the adverse consequences of technological transfers upon the domestic population of the Soviet

---

[1] Gershman, *op. cit.*, p. 44.

Union, the dictates of survival (let alone morality) would indicate a change of course. Western capitalists in particular have to ponder the 20-year-old warning of the German liberal economist Wilhelm Röpke:

'There are but few who stop to think whether in [East-West trade] their business interests are not in conflict with overall political interests . . . which are a matter of life and death for all of us and most of all for Western "capitalists".'[1]

---

[1] Röpke, *op. cit.*, p. 140.

Recommended Reading

Economics

Sutton, Antony C., *Western Technology and Soviet Economic Development 1917-1965*, 3 Vols., Hoover Institution Publications, 1973.

Keller, Werner, *Are the Russians Ten Feet Tall ?*, Thames & Hudson, 1961.

Nove, Alec, *The Soviet Economic System*, George Allen & Unwin, 1977.

Nutter, G. Warren, *The Growth of Industrial Production in the Soviet Union*, National Bureau of Economic Research, Princeton University Press, 1962.

Jasny, Naum, *Soviet Industrialisation 1928-1952*, University of Chicago Press, 1961.

Chapman, Janet, *Real Wages in Soviet Russia since 1928*, Harvard University Press, 1963.

Hayek, F. A. (ed.), *Collectivist Economic Planning*, Routledge & Kegan Paul, Sixth Impression, 1963.

Zemtsov, Ilja, *La Corruption en Union Sovietique*, Hachette, Paris, 1976.

Pejovich, Svetozar, *Life In The Soviet Union: A Report Card on Socialism*, The Fisher Institute, Dallas, Texas, 1979.

Levinson, Charles, *Vodka-Cola,* Gordon & Cremonesi, London, 1979.

Other

Schapiro, L. B., *The Government and Politics of the Soviet Union*, Hutchinson, London, 1965 (6th Edn. 1977).

Szamuely, Tibor, *The Russian Tradition*, Secker & Warberg, 1974.

Solzhenitsyn, Alexander, *The Gulag Archipelago* (3 Vols.), Fontana-Collins, 1977.

Barron, John, *The KGB*, Bantam Books, 1976.

Sakharov, Andrei, *My Country and the World,* Collins, 1975.

Bukovsky, Vladimir, *To Build A Castle*, André Deutsch, 1978.

A Select IEA Bibliography

Rise of the Russian Consumer
A study of the Khrushchev era and the liberalisation of the Russian economy since Stalin
Margaret Miller
1965   40p   Case-bound £1·00
'An invaluable paperback . . . which, better than any book known to me, gives the answers in perfectly straightforward and non-technical language to pretty well all the questions I have ever been asked about the state of perpetual crisis in the Soviet economy . . . Dr Miller has provided a commentary on the issues at stake which, I think, will be a revelation to all those who have so far depended on casual glimpses of the highlights. This is why I think her book is news . . . Here in these pages, most sympathetically presented, we may see the size of the problem. And here, in industry and trade and distribution, we see the very real efforts of the leadership to escape from the consequences of their dogma while yet retaining their faith.'   Edward Crankshaw, *Observer*

Economic Devolution in Eastern Europe
Ljubo Sirc
1969   £1·00
'In this wide-ranging and somewhat discursive account of the economics of East European Communism, Dr Sirc argues that "Reforms became necessary when it transpired that the old Stalinist Soviet model was very inefficient . . . It produces goods nobody wants to buy, establishes productive capacities which cannot be used, keeps personal consumption very low, and causes foreign trade difficulties" .'   *Banker*

Protectionism Again . . . ?
David Greenaway and Christopher Milner
1979   £1·50
'The increasingly vocal arguments for protection of British industry are strongly criticised in a study published today . . . The authors examine tariffs as a way to correct market failures, paying particular attention to the infant industry argument.'   *Financial Times*

Prime Mover of Progress
The Entrepreneur in Capitalism and Socialism
Israel Kirzner, Leslie Hannah, Neil McKendrick, Nigel Vinson, Keith Wickenden, Sir Arthur Knight, Sir Frank McFadzean, P. D. Henderson, D. G. MacRae, Ivor Pearce
1980   £3·50
'This is a timely study which has some considerable relevance to Mrs Thatcher's views on the need for individual incentives etc, in resuscitating the UK economy.'
Professor A. R. Ilersic, *Accountancy*

61

Recent IEA Publications

Hobart Paper 87

1980s Unemployment and the Unions
The Distortion of Relative Prices by Monopoly in the Labour Market
F. A. Hayek
1980   £1·50

'Nobel prize-winning economist Professor Hayek says that Britain would be better off without trade unions, which he regards as the main cause of the country's economic ill-health and high unemployment. In a lengthy condemnation of the "sacred cow" Professor Hayek says that the unions are the prime source of unemployment and the main reason for the decline of the British economy.'   *Guardian*

Hobart Paper 88

Monopoly in Money and Inflation
The Case for a Constitution to Discipline Government
H. Geoffrey Brennan and James M. Buchanan
1981   £1·50

'The authors discuss four schemes whose rules would amount to a form of monetary constitution. But they believe that, as a first step, agreement on the need for a constitution is more important than its precise content.'   *Accountant*

Occasional Paper 59

What is Wrong with the European Communities?
Eleventh Wincott Memorial Lecture
Juergen B. Donges
1981   £1·00

'The Common Agricultural Policy is an absurdity and a scandal, which has been shaped "with an astounding neglect of fundamental economic rules", according to a prominent West German economist.'   *Daily Telegraph*

HOBART PAPERS in print